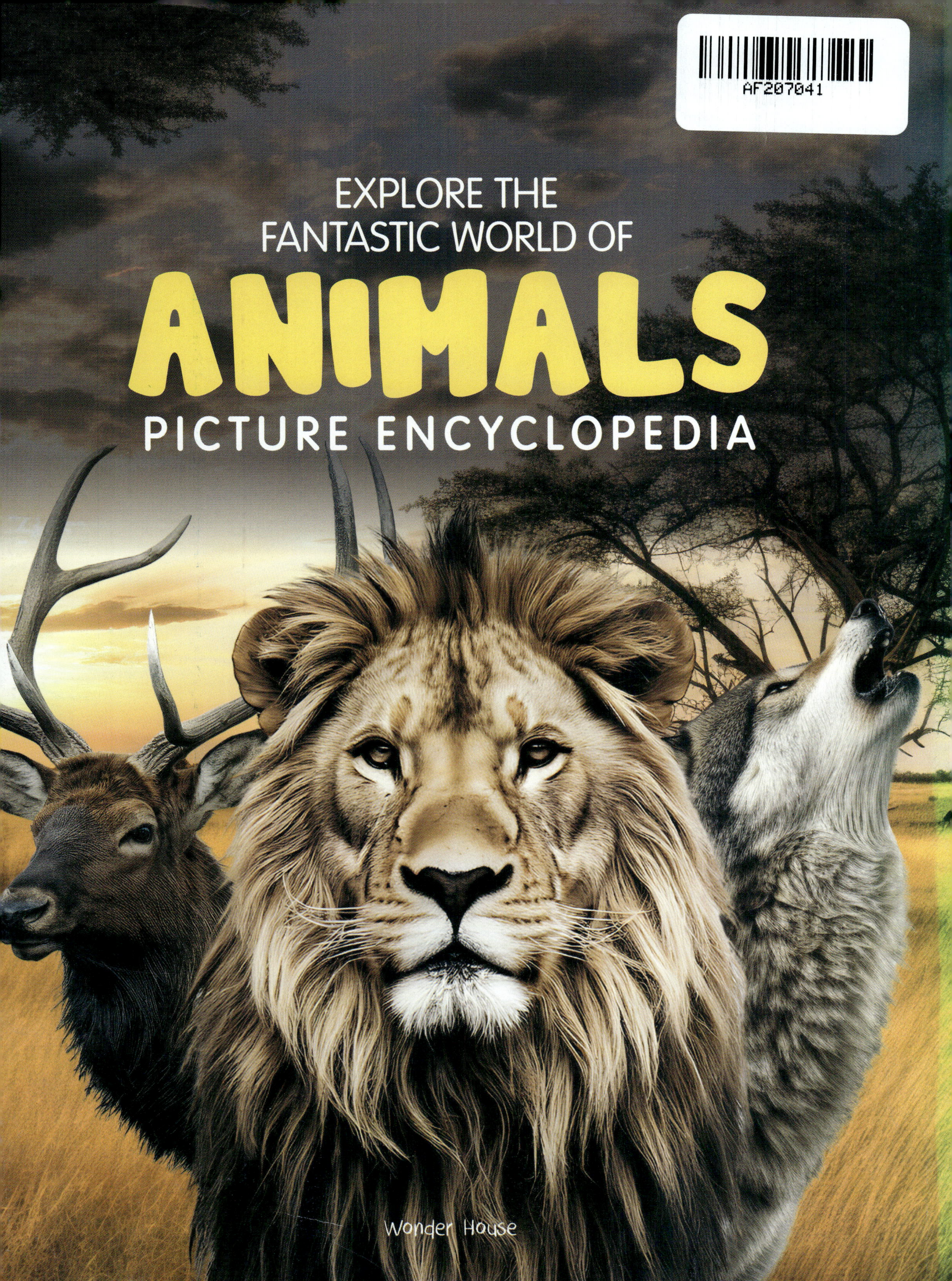
EXPLORE THE
FANTASTIC WORLD OF
ANIMALS
PICTURE ENCYCLOPEDIA
Wonder House

LION

The Lion is a big, strong cat found in Africa and India. Males are especially famous for their impressive manes. Lions have powerful bodies and can weigh from 260–550lb (118–250kg). They grow up to 8ft long (2.5m) from their head to tail. Lions are fast runners and can reach speeds of up to 50mph (80kph) in short bursts. They usually live around 10–16 years in the wild. Lions live in groups called prides and are known for their teamwork. Their scientific name is ***Panthera leo***.

DID YOU KNOW?

Lions spend up to 20 hours a day resting and sleeping.

GIRAFFE

The Giraffe is the tallest animal in the world. They live in Africa and can weigh from 2,000–4,200lb (907–1,905kg). Giraffes can grow up to 18ft (5.5m) tall. They can run as fast as 37mph (60kph) for short distances. Giraffes live around 20–25 years in the wild. They use their long necks to reach high branches for food. Their scientific name is ***Giraffa camelopardalis***.

DID YOU KNOW?

A Giraffe's heart is about 2ft (0.6m) long and weighs around 25lb (11kg).

ZEBRA

The Zebra is a cool, striped animal that lives in Africa. They have black-and-white stripes that help them blend in with their herd. Zebras weigh up to 1,000lb (454kg) and are about 4–5ft (1.2–1.5m) tall at the shoulder. They can run up to 40mph (64kph) to escape predators. Zebras live for around 20 years in the wild. The scientific name of the most widespread Zebra species, Plains Zebra, is ***Equus quagga***.

DID YOU KNOW?

Each Zebra has unique black-and-white stripes, like a fingerprint for humans.

AFRICAN BUFFALO

The African Buffalo is a large and strong animal found in Africa's grasslands and savannas. They can weigh from 660–1,840lb (300–835kg) and stand up to 5.6ft (1.7m) tall at the shoulder. Wild buffaloes are herbivores. They can run up to 37mph (60kph) when threatened. Wild buffaloes can live around 11–22 years in the wild. Their scientific name is ***Syncerus caffer***.

DID YOU KNOW?

They spend most of their day eating grass, which helps maintain the plains/grasslands.

BISON

The Bison is a large, powerful animal that lives in North America and Europe. They have a shaggy mane, a hump on their shoulders and a broad head. Bisons can weigh up to 2,200lb (998kg) and grow up to 6.5ft (2m) tall at the shoulder. Despite their size, Bisons can run up to 40mph (64kph). They can live around 20 years in the wild. The scientific name of American Bison is ***Bison bison***, and that of European Bison is ***Bison bonasus***.

DID YOU KNOW?

Bisons like to roll in the dirt to keep bugs away and to cool off, which is called a "dust bath."

ELEPHANT

The Elephant is the largest land animal in the world! They weigh up to 14,000lb (6350kg) and stand 8–13ft (2.5–4m) tall. They can run up to 25mph (40kph) and live for about 60–70 years. Besides savannas, Elephants also live in forests. They eat grasses, fruits and tree bark. Elephants play an important role in spreading seeds and shaping the land. Humans also value them for their strength and beauty. The scientific name of African Savanna Elephant is ***Loxodonta africana***.

DID YOU KNOW?

African Elephants are very intelligent and can recognize themselves in a mirror.

WILDEBEEST

The Wildebeest, also known as gnu, is a large antelope found in Africa. They have strong bodies with sloping backs, and they travel in huge herds. Wildebeests weigh up to 600lb (272kg). They can grow up to 4.5ft (1.4m) tall at the shoulder. These animals are fast runners, reaching speeds of up to 50mph (80kph). Wildebeests can survive up to 20 years in the wild. Their scientific name is ***Connochaetes taurinus***.

DID YOU KNOW?

Wildebeests are famous for their long-distance migrations, where millions of them travel together across Africa in search of food and water.

HYENA

The Hyena is a clever animal known for its strong jaws that can crush bones with ease. They are found in regions of Africa and few parts of Asia. They can weigh from 90–190lb (40–86kg). Hyenas grow to about 2.5–3ft (0.8–0.9m) tall at the shoulder. They can run up to 37mph (60kph) to chase prey. Hyenas live around 20 years in the wild. Their scientific name is ***Crocuta crocuta***.

DID YOU KNOW?

Hyenas are well-known for their shrill laughs, which help them communicate with the pack.

RHINOCEROS

The Rhinoceros is a large, powerful animal known for its thick skin and impressive horns. They can weigh from 1760–7900lb (800–3580kg) and grow about 10–13ft (3–4m) long. Rhinos can run surprisingly fast, reaching speeds of up to 30mph (48kph) over short distances. They usually live for around 35–50 years in the wild. Rhinos prefer habitats like savannas, grasslands and rainforests. Their diet mainly consists of grass, leaves and shrubs, as they are herbivores. The scientific name for the white Rhinoceros is ***Ceratotherium simum***, while the black Rhinoceros is called ***Diceros bicornis***.

DID YOU KNOW?

Rhino horns are not bones but are made of keratin, the same protein that makes up human hair and nails.

MEERKAT

The Meerkat is a small, social mammal that belongs to the mongoose family. They weigh not more than 2.2lb (1kg) and are about 10–12in (25–30cm) long. Meerkats can run up to 18.6mph (30kph) to escape predators. They typically live for about 7–12 years in the wild. Meerkats thrive in savannas and grasslands, where they dig burrows to stay safe. They can adapt to almost every habitat. They eat insects and plants. Their scientific name is ***Suricata suricatta***.

DID YOU KNOW?

In a Meerkat mob, some stay to care for the young, while others hunt.

CHEETAH

The Cheetah is a slender, agile big cat known for its incredible speed. They typically weigh around 75–140lb (34–64kg) and have a long body about 4–4.5ft (122–137cm) with a tail measuring about 2.5ft (76cm). Cheetahs can run up to 60–70mph (96–112kph), making them the fastest land animals! They usually live for 10–12 years in the wild. Cheetahs prefer open grasslands and savannas where they can spot prey easily. Their diet mainly consists of gazelles and rabbits. The unique black tear marks emerging from the corner of their eyes help reduce the sun's glare while hunting! Their scientific name is ***Acinonyx jubatus***.

DID YOU KNOW?

Unlike other big cats, Cheetahs can't roar, but they make chirping sounds and purrs to communicate.

KANGAROO

The Kangaroo is a unique and iconic animal native to Australia, known for its powerful hind legs that enable it to hop great distances. Kangaroos can weigh up to 200lb (90kg) and stand up to 6ft (1.8m) tall. They are herbivores, eating grass, leaves and other vegetation. Kangaroos can reach speeds of up to 35mph (56kph) when hopping at full speed. They can live around 6–8 years in the wild. Kangaroos are also known for carrying their babies, called joeys, in a pouch on their belly. They belong to the genus ***Macropus***.

DID YOU KNOW?

Kangaroos can jump up to 10ft (3m) in a single bound.

ELK

The Elk is a large, majestic animal found in forests and grasslands across North America and parts of Asia. Elks weigh from 500–1,100lb (225–500kg) and can stand up to 5ft (1.5m) tall at the shoulder. They eat grasses, leaves and tree bark, making them herbivores. Elks can run fast, reaching speeds of up to 45mph (72kph) to escape predators. They live around 10–15 years in the wild. Male Elks, called bulls, are known for their impressive horns called antlers. These antlers fall off and regrow every year. Their scientific name is ***Cervus canadensis***.

DID YOU KNOW?

Elks live in groups called herds, which can include up to 400 individuals.

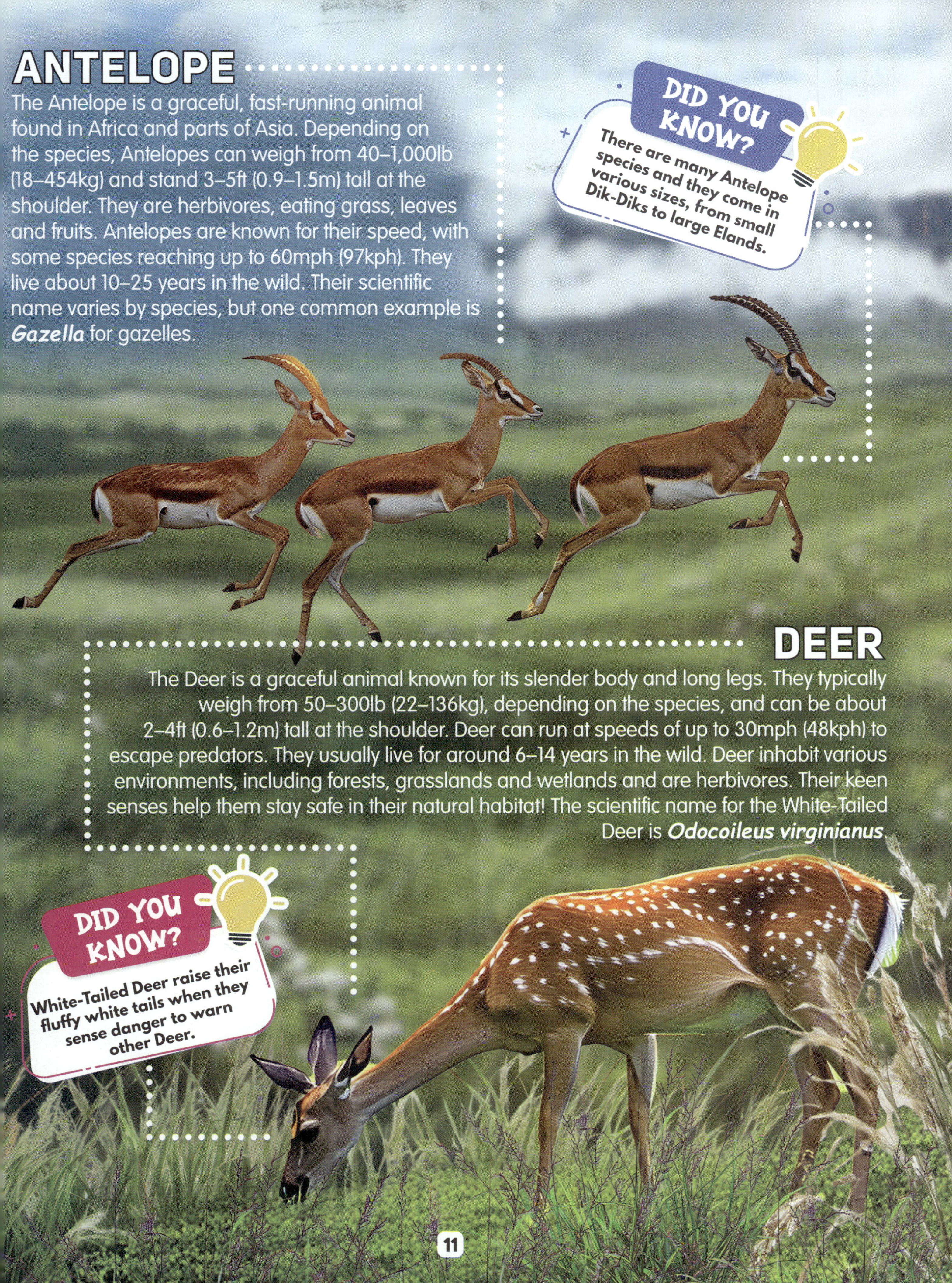

ANTELOPE

The Antelope is a graceful, fast-running animal found in Africa and parts of Asia. Depending on the species, Antelopes can weigh from 40–1,000lb (18–454kg) and stand 3–5ft (0.9–1.5m) tall at the shoulder. They are herbivores, eating grass, leaves and fruits. Antelopes are known for their speed, with some species reaching up to 60mph (97kph). They live about 10–25 years in the wild. Their scientific name varies by species, but one common example is ***Gazella*** for gazelles.

DID YOU KNOW?

There are many Antelope species and they come in various sizes, from small Dik-Diks to large Elands.

DEER

The Deer is a graceful animal known for its slender body and long legs. They typically weigh from 50–300lb (22–136kg), depending on the species, and can be about 2–4ft (0.6–1.2m) tall at the shoulder. Deer can run at speeds of up to 30mph (48kph) to escape predators. They usually live for around 6–14 years in the wild. Deer inhabit various environments, including forests, grasslands and wetlands and are herbivores. Their keen senses help them stay safe in their natural habitat! The scientific name for the White-Tailed Deer is ***Odocoileus virginianus***.

DID YOU KNOW?

White-Tailed Deer raise their fluffy white tails when they sense danger to warn other Deer.

AFRICAN WILD DOG

The African Wild Dog, also known as painted dog, is a social and agile hunter with large, rounded ears. They typically weigh around 40–80lb (18–36kg) and measure about 30–43in (76–109cm) in length excluding their tails. These dogs can run at speeds of up to 40mph (64kph). Wild dogs usually live around 10–12 years in the wild. They prefer open savannahs, grasslands and woodland areas. Their diet mainly consists of Antelope and other small to medium-sized mammals. Their scientific name is ***Lycaon pictus***.

DID YOU KNOW?

Wild Dogs, unlike others of the dog family, have 4 toes instead of 5.

WARTHOG

The Warthog is a unique wild pig found in Africa, known for its distinct tusks and large, flat head. They typically weigh around 120–250lb (54–113kg) and can reach lengths of 3–5ft (0.9–1.5m). Warthogs can run at speeds of up to 30mph (48kph) when they need to escape danger. They usually live around 12–15 years in the wild. Warthogs prefer savannas, grasslands and woodlands, where they dig for food. Their diet mainly consists of grass, roots and berries. The scientific name of the common Warthog is ***Phacochoerus africanus***.

DID YOU KNOW?

Warthogs love to roll in mud to cool off and protect their skin from sunburn and parasites.

COUGAR

The Cougar, also known as mountain lion or puma, is a large, powerful cat that can weigh from 92–220lb (42–100kg). They can grow to about 3–5ft (0.9–1.5m) long, not including their tails, which add about 2–3ft (0.6–0.9m). Cougars are incredibly fast, reaching speeds of up to 30mph (48kph) in short bursts. They can live for around 10–12 years in the wild. Other than savannas, Cougars are found in forests and mountains. Their diet mainly consist of Deer, but they also eat smaller animals. Their scientific name is ***Puma concolor***.

DID YOU KNOW?

Cougars have the largest range of any wild cat in the Americas, from Canada to the southern Andes in South America.

TIGER

The Tiger is a powerful and large wild cat known for its beautiful golden-orange coat with black stripes. Tigers usually weigh from 220–660lb (100–300kg), depending on the species. They can grow up to 10ft (3m) long, including their tail. Tigers are incredibly fast, running at speeds of up to 40mph (64kph). They can live for about 10–11 years in the wild. Tigers live in forests, grasslands and wetlands across Asia. Tigers are skilled hunters with strong jaws, sharp claws and excellent night vision, helping them catch their prey. They mainly eat large animals like Deer, Wild Boar and Buffalo. Their scientific name is ***Panthera tigris***.

DID YOU KNOW?

A Tiger's roar can be heard 1.8mi (3km) away.

BLACK PANTHER

The Black Panther is a stealthy, powerful big cat known for its sleek, black fur. They aren't a separate species but usually a Leopard or Jaguar with a dark coat. Black Panthers weigh from 110–330lb (50–150kg) and can grow up to 8ft (2.4m) in length, including their tail. They can run up to 50mph (80kph). They live about 12–15 years in the wild. Black Panthers eat meat, including Deer, birds and smaller animals. Their scientific name is ***Panthera pardus***, if Leopards or ***Panthera onca***, if Jaguars.

DID YOU KNOW?

They are excellent climbers and are called "ghosts of the forest."

JAGUAR

The Jaguar is a powerful, spotted big cat found in the rainforests of Central and South America. Unlike leopards, which are found in Africa and Asia, Jaguars have larger, more rounded spots with a central dot and are known for their strong bite, which can crush bones. Jaguars weigh from 100–350lb (45–159kg) and can grow up to 6ft (1.8m) long, not including their tail. They are carnivores, eating animals like Deer, fish and even Caimans. Jaguars can run up to 50mph (80kph) in short bursts and live around 12–15 years in the wild. Their scientific name is ***Panthera onca***.

DID YOU KNOW?

Jaguars are important in the mythology of many South American cultures, often seen as symbols of power and protection.

SLOTH

The Sloth is a slow-moving animal with a speed of about 0.1mph (0.2kph). They live in the trees of Central and South America. Sloths are known for their lazy and sluggish lifestyle and hang upside down in trees. They weigh around 8–17lb (3.6–7.7kg) and can grow up to 2.5ft (76cm) long. They live around 20–30 years. Their scientific name is ***Folivora***, and they mainly eat leaves, fruit and twigs.

DID YOU KNOW?

Sloths have a slow metabolism, and it can take them a whole month to digest a single meal!

LEMUR

The Lemur is a unique primate found only on the islands of Madagascar. They typically weigh from 5–8lb (2.2–3.6kg) and measure about 4–28in (10–71cm) long, excluding their long tails. These agile animals can leap between trees and are known for their playful nature. Lemurs usually live around 15–20 years in the wild. They inhabit rainforests, dry forests and wetlands, feeding mainly on fruits, leaves and flowers. The scientific name for the Ring-Tailed Lemur is ***Lemur catta***.

DID YOU KNOW?

Some Lemurs can leap up to 30ft (9.1m) in a single jump!

PANDA

The Panda is a lovable Bear known for its black-and-white fur and gentle nature. Pandas live in the bamboo forests of China. They weigh around 220–330lb (100–150kg) and grow up to 5ft (1.5m) long. Though not very fast, they can climb trees and swim well. Pandas live around 20 years in the wild. Pandas mainly eat bamboo, munching on it for most of the day. Their scientific name is ***Ailuropoda melanoleuca***.

DID YOU KNOW?

Pandas can climb as high as 13,000ft (3,962m).

GRAY WOLF

The Wolf is a fascinating wild animal known for its strong body and pack behavior. The most well-known and commonly found Wolf is the Gray Wolf. They typically weigh around 40–150lb (18–68kg) and can be about 4.5–6.5ft (1.3–2m) long, including their bushy tails. Wolves can run at speeds of up to 40mph (64kph) over short distances. They usually live for around 6–8 years in the wild. Gray Wolves prefer habitats like tundras and grasslands. Their diet mainly consists of large prey, such as Deer and Elk. Their scientific name is ***Canis lupus***.

DID YOU KNOW?

Wolves communicate by howling, which can be heard even 10 miles away.

JACKAL

The Jackal is a medium-sized canine known for its slender body and bushy tail. They typically weigh around 15–25lb (6.8–11.3kg) and measure about 35in (89cm) long. Jackals can run at speeds of up to 20mph (32kph). Their lifespan in the wild is around 10–12 years. Jackals live in a variety of habitats, including savannas, deserts and grasslands. They are omnivorous, eating small mammals, plants and insects. Golden Jackals and Black-Backed Jackals are named after their fur color. The scientific name for the Black-Backed Jackal is ***Canis mesomelas***.

DID YOU KNOW?

Jackals often follow lions on hunt to feed on their leftovers.

RED FOX

The Fox is a small to medium-sized mammal known for its bushy tail and pointed ears. Red Fox is the most common species among others. They typically weigh around 5–24lb (2–11kg) and can range in size from 18–35in (45–89cm) long. Foxes are quick, capable of running at speeds of up to 30mph (48kph). They usually live around 3–5 years in the wild. Foxes are adaptable and can be found in forests, grasslands and urban areas. Their diet consists of small mammals, birds, fruits and insects. Their scientific name is ***Vulpes vulpes***.

DID YOU KNOW?

Foxes are clever and use tricks to catch their prey, like pretending to be dead.

LEOPARD

The Leopard is a big, strong cat with a sleek, spotted coat that helps it blend into the wild. Leopards weigh from 60–200lb (27–90kg) and can grow up to 4–6.3ft (1.2–1.9m) long, not including their tail. They are incredibly fast, reaching speeds of up to 36mph (58kph). Leopards can live around 12–17 years in the wild. They live in various habitats, including forests, mountains, grasslands and deserts. Leopards eat a wide range of animals, such as Antelopes, Deer and small mammals. They're skilled hunters and are great at climbing trees. Their scientific name is ***Panthera pardus***.

DID YOU KNOW?

Leopards are excellent climbers and often take their prey up on the trees to keep it for themselves.

RED PANDA

The Red Panda is a small, furry animal with reddish-brown fur and a bushy tail, native to the forests of the Himalayas and China. They weigh around 7–15lb (3–7kg) and grow about 20–26in (51–66cm) long, not including their tail. Red Pandas mostly eat bamboo, but they also enjoy fruits, berries and insects. They move slowly and can climb well. Red Pandas live around 8–10 years in the wild. They are known for their playful nature and love for tree branches. Their scientific name is ***Ailurus fulgens***.

DID YOU KNOW?

Even though they share a name, Red Pandas are not closely related to Giant Pandas.

KOALA

The Koala is a cute, furry animal with a round face and large, fluffy ears. Popularly known as Koala Bears, they are in fact related to Kangaroos. They have thick, soft fur that's usually gray with a white belly. Koalas weigh up to 30lb (14kg) and grow to about 24–33in (61–84cm) long. They move slowly, around 6.2mph (10kph), and live for about 15–20 years. Koalas live in the eucalyptus forests in Australia, spending most of their time on trees. They eat eucalyptus leaves and their scientific name is ***Phascolarctos cinereus***.

DID YOU KNOW?

Koalas have fingerprints like humans. Even under the microscope, they look almost the same!

BEAR

The Bear is a large mammal, known for its stout body and powerful limbs. They can weigh from 60–1,600lb (27–725kg), depending on the species. Bears typically stand about 3–10ft (0.9–3m) tall when on their hind legs. Despite their size, they can run up to 30mph (48kph)! In the wild, Bears live around 20–30 years. They inhabit forests, mountains and tundras across North America, Europe and Asia. Bears are omnivores, eating fruits, nuts, fish and small animals. They belong to the family ***Ursidae***. The most common Bear species are the American Black Bears, scientifically known as ***Ursus americanus***, and the Brown Bears or ***Ursus arctos***.

DID YOU KNOW?

Brown Bears have an incredible sense of smell, even better than a dog's! They can smell food from miles away.

GIBBON APE

The Gibbon is a small, agile ape known for swinging quickly through trees. Gibbons are found in the forests of Southeast Asia. They weigh from 11–25lb (5–11kg) and have a body length ranging from 16–25in (40–64cm). Gibbons are incredibly fast, swinging from branch to branch at speeds up to 35mph (56kph). They live about 25–30 years in the wild. Gibbons have long arms and are known for their loud, whooping calls. They belong to the family ***Hylobatidae***.

DID YOU KNOW?

Unlike other monkeys, Gibbons don't have tails. They rely on their strong arms for balance while moving across the treetops.

DID YOU KNOW?

The Lynx has cool tufts of black hair on the tips of its ears, which help it hear better and to keep warm.

LYNX

The Lynx is a wild cat with thick fur, pointy ears and a short tail that lives in forests across Europe, Asia and America. They can weigh from 22–44lb (10–20kg) and grow up to 47in (1.2m) long, including their tail. Lynxes can run up to 50mph (80kph) when chasing prey. They usually live around 10–12 years in the wild. The scientific name of Eurasian Lynx is ***Lynx Lynx***.

CHIMPANZEE

The Chimpanzee is a smart, social primate that lives in African forests. They weigh around 70–130lb (32–60kg) and can grow up to 5.5ft (1.7m) tall when standing upright. Chimpanzees are omnivores, eating fruits, nuts, leaves and sometimes insects or small animals. They can move quickly, climbing trees and swing from branches with ease. Chimpanzees live about 45 years in the wild. They are known for using tools like sticks to find food. Their scientific name is ***Pan troglodytes***.

DID YOU KNOW?

Chimpanzees share about 98 percent of their DNA with humans, making them our closest living relatives!

ORANGUTAN

The Orangutan is a large, orange-furred ape that lives in the rainforests of Borneo and Sumatra. Orangutans weigh between 90–200lb (40–90kg) and can grow up to 5ft (1.5m) tall. They are strong climbers, moving slowly through trees using their long arms. Orangutans eat mostly fruit, but also leaves, bark and insects. They live around 30–40 years in the wild. The scientific name is ***Pongo pygmaeus*** for the Bornean Orangutan and ***Pongo abelii*** for the Sumatran Orangutan.

DID YOU KNOW?

Orangutans build big, comfortable nests in trees every night to sleep in.

GORILLA

The Gorilla is a large, gentle primate that lives in the forests of Africa. They are divided into 2 species—Western and Eastern Gorilla. They can weigh between 300–500lb (136–227kg) and stand up to 5.5ft (1.7m) tall when on two legs. Gorillas are mostly herbivores, eating leaves, fruit and stems, but sometimes they eat insects. They move slowly on the ground, walking on their knuckles, but can run up to 25mph (40kph) if needed. Gorillas can live up to 35–40 years in the wild. Gorillas are known for their strong family bonds and gentle nature. The scientific name of Western Gorilla is ***Gorilla Gorilla***.

DID YOU KNOW?

Their arms are longer than their legs, which helps them swing through trees and climb.

HIPPOPOTAMUS

The Hippopotamus, or hippo, is a large, water-loving animal found in Africa. Hippos can weigh from 6,600–8,000lb (2,993–3,629kg) and grow up to 16ft (5m) long. They spend much of their time in rivers and lakes to stay cool. Hippos are herbivores, mainly eating grass and plants, and can eat up to 150lb (68kg) of food a night. Despite their size, they can run up to 30mph (48kph) on land. Hippos can live around 40 years in the wild. Their scientific name is ***Hippopotamus amphibius***.

DID YOU KNOW?

Hippos produce a red, oily substance that acts as sunscreen, protecting their skin from the harmful sun rays.

OTTER

The Otter is a playful wetland animal with a sleek, streamlined body perfect for swimming. They have thick, waterproof fur, webbed feet and a long, strong tail to help them glide through the water. River Otters and Sea Otters make up 13 species of Otters. The mass of River Otters ranges from 11–30lb (5–14kg), and they grow up to 4ft (1.2m) long. They can swim up to 7mph (11kph) and live about 8–10 years. Most Otter species are found in rivers, lakes and marshes and only 2 species in sea. They eat fish, frogs and small invertebrates. Their family name is ***Mustelidae***.

DID YOU KNOW?

River Otters can hold their breath underwater for up to 8 minutes!

CAPYBARA

The Capybara is a large, gentle rodent found in wetlands. They have barrel-shaped bodies with short legs, partially webbed feet, and blunt muzzles. Capybaras can weigh up to 145lb (66kg) and grow to about 4ft (1.2m) long. They can run up to 22mph (35kph) and live around 8 years in the wild. Capybaras live in grassy wetlands and love to swim. They mainly eat grass and aquatic plants. Their scientific name is ***Hydrochoerus hydrochaeris***.

DID YOU KNOW?

Capybaras can sleep in water with just their nose sticking out to breathe.

GREEN VINE SNAKE

The Green Vine Snake is a long, slender snake that looks like a green vine, helping it hide in trees. They weigh around 0.7–1.5oz (20–42g) and can grow up to 6.5ft (2m) long. Green Vine Snakes eat small animals like insects and lizards, which they catch with their quick strikes. They can move swiftly through the trees, but they are not very fast on the ground. They live about 6–8 years in the wild. Green Vine Snakes are found in the rainforests of Southeast Asia. Their scientific name is ***Ahaetulla nasuta***.

DID YOU KNOW?

Despite their scary look, Green Vine Snakes are not venomous and are harmless to humans.

CROCODILE

The Crocodile is a large, powerful reptile found in tropical regions around the world. They can weigh up to 2,200lb (998kg) and grow up to 23ft (7m) long, depending on the species. Crocodiles are carnivores, eating fish, birds and even large mammals. They can run up to 15mph (24kph) on land and swim at about 20mph (32kph) in water. Crocodiles can live 30–70 years in the wild. They live in rivers, lakes and swamps. Their scientific name is ***Crocodylidae***.

PYTHON

The Python is a large, non-venomous snake known for its long, muscular body. Their weight averages around 250lb (113kg), depending on the species. Some Pythons can grow over 20ft (6m) long! They move slowly, but can strike suddenly when hunting. Pythons live up to 20–25 years in the wild. They are found in rainforests, grasslands and swamps in Africa, Asia and Australia. Pythons eat small animals like birds and mammals. The Reticulated Python is one of the largest snakes in the world and its scientific name is ***Python reticulatus***.

DID YOU KNOW?

Iguanas love to bask in the sun to keep warm, so they are often found lounging in sunny spots.

DID YOU KNOW?

When they catch their food, they squeeze it tightly in a special way called constriction, to help them eat.

GREEN IGUANA

The Green Iguana is a fascinating reptile known for its long body and tail. They can weigh up to 13lb (5.9kg). Adult Iguanas can grow up to 5–7ft (1.5–2.1m) long, including their tail. Iguanas can run at speeds of up to 21mph (33.8kph). They can live for around 15–20 years in the wild. They are primarily found in tropical rainforests. Iguanas are herbivores, eating leaves, fruits and flowers. Their scientific name is ***Iguana iguana***.

GHARIAL

The Gharial is a unique crocodile with a long, thin snout filled with sharp teeth, perfect for catching fish. Gharials can weigh up to 2,000lb (907kg) and grow up to 15ft (4.6m) long. They primarily eat fish and are excellent swimmers, using their powerful tails to move quickly through the water. Gharials can live up to 40–60 years in the wild. They are found in the rivers of India and Nepal. Their scientific name is ***Gavialis gangeticus***.

DID YOU KNOW?

An adult male Gharial can grow up to 19ft (5.8m) tall!

CHINESE CROCODILE LIZARD

The Chinese Crocodile Lizard is a unique reptile with a tough, scaly body that resembles a Crocodile. They typically weigh around 7–10oz (198–283g) and grow up to 8–16in (20–41cm) long. These lizards eat insects, worms and small fish. They are slow-moving and prefer to stay still for long periods. Chinese Crocodile Lizards can live up to 10 years in captivity. Their home is in cool, forested areas near water in southern China and northern Vietnam. Their scientific name is ***Shinisaurus crocodilurus***.

DID YOU KNOW?

These lizards can change their color a bit to blend in with their surroundings.

TORTOISE

The Tortoise is a unique reptile known for its hard shells and slow movements. They can weigh anywhere from 100–1,000lb (45–454kg), depending on the species. Most Tortoises have a shell length range from 4–6in (10–15cm) long, but the Galápagos Giant Tortoise, the largest species, can reach a shell length up to 3ft (91.4cm)! Tortoises are not fast, moving at about 0.1–0.2mph (0.2–0.3kph). They can live for 50 to over 100 years. Tortoises live in various habitats, including deserts and wet tropical forests. They are herbivores, feeding on grasses, leaves and fruits. The scientific name for the Galápagos Giant Tortoise is ***Chelonoidis nigra***.

DID YOU KNOW?

Their shell shape can vary depending on their habitat.

TOKAY GECKO

The Tokay Gecko is a large, colorful lizard found in Southeast Asia. They weigh about 5–14oz (150–400g) and grow up to 12–16in (30.5–40.7cm) long. Tokay Geckos eat insects, small animals and sometimes even other Geckos. They are quick climbers and can run fast on walls. They live around 10–20 years in the wild and make their homes in forests and rocky areas. Their scientific name is ***Gekko gecko***.

DID YOU KNOW?

Tokay Geckos have sticky pads on their feet that help them climb walls and even glass!

DID YOU KNOW?

Crocodiles have been around for over 200 million years, which means they existed even when dinosaurs roamed the Earth!

KOMODO DRAGON

The Komodo Dragon is the largest lizard in the world, found on the Indonesian islands of Komodo, Rinca, Flores and Gili Motang. They can weigh up to 300lb (136kg) and grow up to 10ft (3m) long. Komodo Dragons are carnivores, eating meat like Deer, Pigs and even Water Buffalos. They can run up to 12mph (19kph) in short bursts. Komodo Dragons live around 30 years in the wild. Their scientific name is ***Varanus komodoensis***.

DID YOU KNOW?

Their saliva contains large amounts of bacteria, which can make their bite harmful. If they bite their prey, it can get very sick.

FROG

The Frog is a small amphibian with smooth, moist skin and long, powerful hind legs for jumping. They usually weigh around 0.1–1lb (45-453g), depending on the species. Frogs can grow from 0.9–12in (2.3–30.5cm) long. They can leap up to 20 times their body length in a single jump! Frogs typically live for 5–10 years. They live near freshwater, such as ponds, rivers and wetlands. Frogs eat insects and sometimes even small fish. Common Frog species are the American Bullfrog, scientifically called ***Lithobates catesbeianus***, and the Gliding Frog is ***Rhacophorus nigropalmatus***.

DID YOU KNOW?

Gliding Frogs can jump and glide through the air from tree to tree, using their webbed feet to steer like wings!

GREEN TREE VIPER

The Green Tree Viper is a venomous snake known for its vibrant colors and heat-sensing pits. They typically weigh around 1–2lb (0.4–1kg). They grow up to 3ft (91.4cm) long. Tree vipers are not very fast, moving slowly but striking quickly when needed. They live about 10–15 years in the wild. These snakes live in rainforests, often high up in trees. They eat small mammals, birds and frogs. They belong to the genus **Trimeresurus**.

DID YOU KNOW?

The Green Tree Viper has venom that it uses to catch its prey, but it usually avoids humans and only bites if threatened.

CHAMELEON

The Chameleon is an amazing reptile known for its ability to change color to blend in with its surroundings. They usually weigh about 0.5–2oz (14–57g) and can grow up to 27in (68cm) long, depending on the species. Chameleons eat insects like crickets and flies, using their long, sticky tongues to catch them. They move slowly, with a top speed of about 0.5mph (0.8kph). Chameleons can live ranging from a few months to about 10 years depending upon the species. They live in forests and deserts, and their family name is ***Chamaeleonidae***.

DID YOU KNOW?

Their tongues can be twice as long as their body, and they use them to catch insects quickly!

POLAR BEAR

The Polar Bear is a huge, powerful Bear that lives in the Arctic, near the North Pole. They have thick white fur that keeps them warm in the icy cold. They can weigh between 900–1,600lb (408–725kg) and grow up to 8ft (2.4m) long, including their tail. Polar Bears are excellent swimmers and can run up to 25mph (40kph) on land. They mainly eat Seals, which they hunt by waiting near holes in the ice. Polar Bears live about 25–30 years in the wild. Their scientific name is ***Ursus maritimus***.

DID YOU KNOW?

Under their white fur, Polar Bears have black skin that absorbs sunlight and helps keep them warm.

SNOW LEOPARD

The Snow Leopard is a beautiful big cat that lives in the snowy mountains of Asia. They weigh between 60–120lb (27–54kg) and are about 4ft (1.2m) long, excluding the tail, which is about 3ft (0.9m) long. Snow Leopards are excellent climbers and can run up to 35mph (56kph) in short bursts. Snow Leopards eat animals like Mountain Goats, Sheep, Ibex and small rodents. They live around 10–15 years in the wild. Their scientific name is ***Panthera uncia***.

DID YOU KNOW?

The Snow Leopard's unique spots help it to blend in with its rocky environment.

ARCTIC FOX

The Arctic Fox is a small, fluffy animal that lives in the cold Arctic regions. They weigh between 6.5–17lb (3–7.7kg) and are about 18–26in (46–66cm) in length, excluding the tail. They have thick fur to keep them warm in icy temperatures. Arctic Foxes can run up to 30mph (48kph) to catch their prey. They eat rodents, birds and even carrion. Arctic Foxes live around 3–6 years in the wild. Their scientific name is ***Vulpes lagopus***.

DID YOU KNOW?

In summer, their fur turns brown or gray to blend in with the tundra, while in winter, it turns white for camouflage.

CAMEL

The Camel is a large, hardy animal known for its humps, which store fat to help it survive in the desert. They can weigh between 900–1,600lb (408–725kg) and stand about 6–7ft (1.8–2.1m) tall at the hump. Camels eat grass, dry leaves and desert plants. They can run up to 40mph (64kph) in short bursts. Camels can live for 40–50 years. Their home is in deserts, and the scientific name of the One-Humped Dromedary Camel is ***Camelus dromedarius***.

DID YOU KNOW?

Camels store fat in their humps, not water! This helps them go without food for long periods.

FENNEC FOX

The Fennec Fox is the smallest fox in the world, with large ears and a sandy-colored coat that helps it stay cool in the desert. It weighs about 2–3lb (1–1.4kg) and grows to about 9–16in (23–41cm) long, with its big ears measuring up to 6in (15cm). It can run up to 20mph (32kph) and lives for around 10–12 years. The Fennec Fox lives in the sandy deserts of North Africa, eating insects, rodents, small mammals and plants. Its scientific name is ***Vulpes zerda***.

DID YOU KNOW?

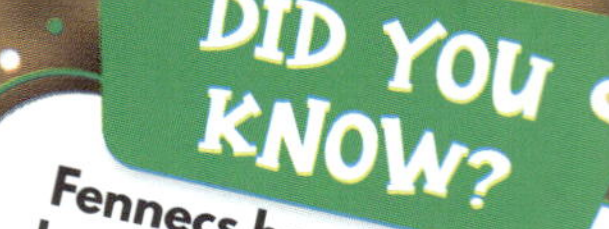

Fennecs have extremely hairy body and feet, The hair on the feet protect them from the extremely hot sands.

BIGHORN SHEEP

The Bighorn Sheep is a wild animal known for its large, curved horns. Desert bighorns are one of the many subspecies. They weigh from 150–300lb (68–136kg) and stand about 3–3.5ft (0.9–1.1m) tall at the shoulder. Bighorn Sheep eat grasses, shrubs and plants found in rocky mountain areas. They can run up to 20mph (32kph) and are excellent climbers. They live around 10–15 years in the wild. Their home is in the mountains of North America, and their scientific name is ***Ovis canadensis***.

DID YOU KNOW?

Bighorn Sheep are amazing climbers. They can easily scale steep, rocky mountainsides, thanks to their special hooves that grip the rocks.

DOG

The Dog is a friendly and loyal pet that comes in many shapes and sizes! They can weigh anywhere from 5–200lb (2–90kg) depending on the breed. Most Dogs range from about 5–30in (13–76cm) tall at the shoulder. They can run at speeds of up to 45mph (72kph), making them great companions for playtime. Dogs typically live around 10–15 years. They can adapt to various habitats, including homes, backyards and parks. Dogs are omnivores, enjoying foods like Dog kibble, meat, vegetables and treats. The scientific name for a domestic Dog is ***Canis lupus familiaris***.

DID YOU KNOW?

Golden Retrievers often work as therapy animals because of their gentle and caring nature.

CAT

The Domestic Cat is a popular pet known for its playful and independent nature. They typically weigh around 5–20lb (2.3–9kg) and are about 5–17in (12.7–43cm) long. Cats eat a diet of Cat food, including meat and fish. They can run up to 30mph (48kph) in short bursts. Cats usually live around 15 years. Their scientific name is ***Felis Catus***.

DID YOU KNOW?

Just like human fingerprints, every cat has a unique nose print. No two cats have the same pattern on their noses!

HAMSTER

The Hamster is a small, cute rodent that makes a great pet. They usually weigh about 4oz (113g) and grow about 4–7in (10–18cm) long. Hamsters eat seeds, fruits and vegetables, enjoying a mix of Hamster food. They are quick runners, reaching speeds of up to 6mph (9.6kph) on their wheels. Hamsters live around 2–3 years. They live in cages with bedding and tunnels. The scientific name of Golden Hamster is ***Mesocricetus auratus***.

DID YOU KNOW?

Hamsters have special cheek pouches where they store food to eat later. They can stuff a lot of food in these pockets!

SHEEP

The Domestic Sheep is a fluffy, gentle animal known for its woolly coats. They typically weigh between 100–350lb (45–159kg) and stand about 2–4ft (0.6–1.2m) tall at the shoulder. Sheep eat grass, hay and grains, grazing in fields. They aren't very fast, usually running up to 25mph (40kph) when needed. Sheep live around 10–12 years. Their home is in farms and pastures. Their scientific name is ***Ovis aries***.

DID YOU KNOW?

Sheep have rectangular pupils.

GOAT

The Domestic Goat is a friendly and curious animal often kept on farms. They typically weigh around 100–120lb (45–54kg) and can stand about 2–3ft (0.6–0.9m) tall at the shoulder. Goats eat grass, hay and leaves, and they love to nibble on almost anything! They can run up to 10mph (16kph). Goats live around for 15 years. Their home is usually a barn or field. Their scientific name is ***Capra hircus***.

DID YOU KNOW?

Goats wag their tails when they're happy or excited, just like how dogs wag their tails!

COW

The Cow is a gentle, strong animal that is very important to farms. They can weigh from 800–2,400lb (362–1088kg) and stand about 4–5ft (1.2–1.5m) tall at the shoulder. Cows eat mostly grass, hay and grains. Although they are not fast, Cows can trot at speeds up to 25mph (40kph). Cows live for about 15–20 years and are usually found on farms. They belong to the species of domestic cattle, ***Bos taurus***. Cows have beautiful, large eyes and soft, short hair.

DID YOU KNOW?

A Cow's tongue is very long and rough, which helps it pull leaves and grass into its mouths.

HORSE

The Horse is a strong and fast animal known for its grace and beauty. They can weigh between 400–2,000lb (181–907kg) depending on the breed (Ponies, racing Horse, etc) and can grow up to 5–6ft (1.5–1.8m) tall at the shoulder. Horses can run up to 55mph (88kph) in short bursts and live for about 20–35 years. Their bodies are built with long legs and powerful muscles, making them great runners. Horses used to live and roam freely in grasslands but are now mostly domesticated. For thousands of years they have been helping humans with transport, farming and companionship. They eat grasses, hay and grains. Their scientific name is ***Equus caballus***.

DID YOU KNOW?

Horses can sleep standing up! They have a special way of locking their legs so they don't fall over.

YAK

The Yak is a large, strong animal that lives in the cold, high mountains of Asia, specifically in Tibet. They are also found in parts of Nepal and Mongolia. Yaks of the wild weigh up to 2,200lb (998kg), though the domestic ones weigh much less. They can grow up to 6.5ft (2m). Yaks eat grass, plants and shrubs. They can run up to 25mph (40kph) for short distances and live about 25 years in captivity. Yaks are important to people for their milk, meat, wool and are pack animals. Their scientific name is ***Bos grunniens***.

DID YOU KNOW?

Yaks have big, round eyes and large ears to help them see and hear well in their snowy, windy home.

LLAMA

The Llama is a friendly, domesticated animal known for its unique appearance and gentle nature. They typically weigh about 250–450lb (113–204kg). Llamas stand about 3–4ft (0.9–1.2m) tall at the shoulder. They can run at speeds of up to 35mph (56kph) in short bursts. Llamas usually live for 15–20 years. They are found in the Andes Mountains of South America. Llamas are herbivores, primarily eating grass and other plants. Their scientific name is ***Lama glama***.

DID YOU KNOW?

Llamas belong to the camel family though they lack humps, a unique feature of the camel.

SQUIRREL

The Squirrel is a small mammal that makes a delightful pet! They usually weigh between 0.1–7lb (0.04–3kg) and can grow about 6–36in (15–91cm) long, including their bushy tails. Squirrels can run at speeds of up to 20mph (32kph), making them quick and playful. They typically live around 6–12 years in captivity. Squirrels prefer habitats like forests and parks, where they can climb trees and find food. They eat nuts, seeds, fruits and vegetables. Their energetic nature and cute antics make them fun companions! The scientific name for the most common pet Squirrel, the Eastern Grey Squirrel, is ***Sciurus carolinensis***.

DID YOU KNOW?

There are over 200 species of Squirrels around the world, including Tree Squirrels, Ground Squirrels and Flying Squirrels!

RABBIT

The Rabbit is a soft, furry animal that makes a great pet. They usually weigh around 1–5lb (0.4–2.2kg) and can grow up to 20in (51cm) long, depending on the breed. Rabbits love to eat hay, fresh vegetables and specially made Rabbit pellets. They can run fast, reaching speeds of up to 45mph (72kph) when they're excited. Rabbits can live for about 8–12 years under domestic care. They live in cozy cages or hutches with plenty of room to hop around. The scientific name of the European rabbit, the most common pet, is ***Oryctolagus cuniculus***.

DID YOU KNOW?

A Rabbit's teeth keep growing throughout its life, so they need to chew on things like hay and carrots to keep them trimmed.

WHITE RAT

The White Rat is a small, friendly pet with a lot of personality. They typically weigh around 0.5–1lb (0.2–0.4kg) and grow about 9–11in (23–28cm) long, not including their tail. They are quick movers, running up to 8mph (13kph). White Rats live around 2–3 years and are often kept in cages in homes. They eat seeds, grains, fruits and vegetables. White rats are used by scientists for research and are also loved for their playful and social nature. Their scientific name is ***Rattus norvegicus domestica***.

DID YOU KNOW?

White Rats are very smart and can learn tricks, navigate mazes and even recognize their names.

FERRET

The Ferret is a small, playful animal with long, slender body. They weigh about 2lb (1kg) and grow about 15–20in (38–51cm) long. Ferrets eat meat, such as small rodents or specially made Ferret food. They are quick and can run up to 16mph (25kph). Ferrets can live up to 12 years under a protected shelter and are often kept as pets. Historically, Ferrets were used to hunt rodents and help control pests. The scientific name of the common Ferret is ***Mustela putorius furo***.

DID YOU KNOW?

When Ferrets move around, they often wiggle their bodies and slink low to the ground. This is called the "weasel war dance."

HEDGEHOG

The Hedgehog is a small, spiky animal that makes an interesting pet. They usually weigh up to 1.5lb (0.7kg) and grow to about 5–12in (13–30cm) long. Hedgehogs eat insects, fruits and vegetables. They can run up to 4mph (6kph) and live around 4–7 years. Hedgehogs are often found in gardens or homes as pets. Hedgehogs help control insect populations and are beloved for their cute, curious nature. The scientific name of the Western European hedgehog is ***Erinaceus europaeus***.

DID YOU KNOW?

Hedgehogs have about 5,000–7,000 tiny spines on their backs that help protect them from predators.